Reflecting Light

Louise and Richard
Spilsbury

Heinemann
raintree

Edited by Penny West
Designed by Rich Parker
Original illustrations © Capstone Global Library Ltd 2015
Illustrated by HL Studios
Picture research by Tracy Cummins
Production by Helen McCreath
Originated by Capstone Global Library Ltd
Printed and bound in China by CTPS

19 18 17 16 15
10 9 8 7 6 5 4 3 2 1

Library of Congress Cataloging-in-Publication Data
Spilsbury, Louise, author.
  Reflecting light / Louise Spilsbury and Richard Spilsbury.—[1st edition].
    pages cm.—(Exploring light)
  Summary: "This book looks at what reflections are and how we can use them. - Mirrors reflect light back at exactly the same angle. You can make a "mirror book" to explore symmetry and multiple reflections. - Why does a straight straw look bent in a glass of water? Experiment using air, oil, and water to see how different materials affect the speed of light. - Look at how our eyes use reflected light to see and make a pinhole camera to show how the eye works. And much more!"—Provided by publisher.
  Includes bibliographical references and index.
  ISBN 978-1-4109-7943-8 (hb)—ISBN 978-1-4109-7948-3 (pb)— ISBN 978-1-4109-7958-2 (ebook) 1. Reflection (Optics)—Juvenile literature. 2. Light—Scattering—Juvenile literature. 3. Lenses—Juvenile literature. I. Spilsbury, Richard, 1963- author. II. Title.
  QC425.2.S65 2016
  535.323—dc23   2014039856

This book has been officially leveled by using the F&P Text Level Gradient™ Leveling System.

Acknowledgments
The author and publisher are grateful to the following for permission to reproduce copyright material:
Capstone Press: HL Studios, 15, 19, 23, 8, 9, 12, 13, 14, 16, 17, 20, 21, 24, 25, 28, 29; Getty Images: AFP/Krister Soerboe, 11, 26, David Woolley, Cover; iStockphoto: Kali Nine LLC, 4; Shutterstock: agsandrew, Design Element, ALMAGAMI, Design Element, bikeriderlondon, 10, Blend Images, 22, Click Bestsellers, Design Element, Dennis Tokarzewski, Design Element, Elena Elisseeva, 7, ID1974, Design Element, Lisa F. Young, 27, luckypic, Design Element, Samson Yury, 18, Steve Bower, 6, Vass Zoltan, Design Element, Vitaliy Krasovskiy, 5.

We would like to thank Catherine Jones for her invaluable help in the preparation of this book.

007370CTPSF15

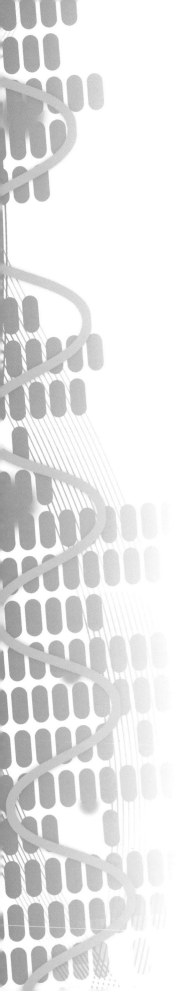

Contents

Some words are shown in bold, **like this**. You can find out what they mean by looking in the glossary.

Reflecting Light

We can only see most of the things around us because light **reflects** off them. If you bounce a ball against a wall, the ball bounces back. When light hits a surface, it bounces back, too. During the day, we see grass, trees, and other things outdoors because light from the Sun bounces off them into our eyes. When it is dark, the light from flashlights, lamps, and other **light sources** reflects off objects so we can see them.

In the day, we see the things around us when sunlight reflects off them.

The tree is not inside this building. It is across from it. It is reflected in the building's windows.

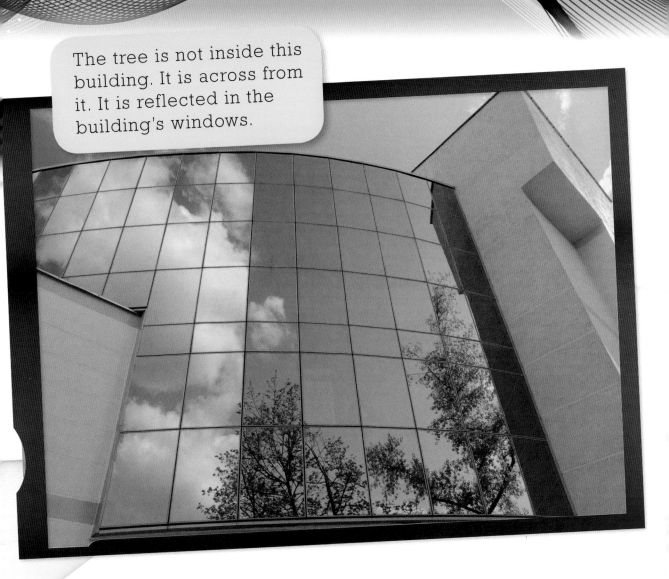

Did you look in the mirror when you brushed your teeth today? When light reflects off some surfaces, it creates a **reflection**. When you look in a mirror, you see a reflection of your own face looking back at you. Sometimes we see reflections of trees, buildings, and other objects in the water of a pond or a lake.

Reflections

Take a walk around and see where you can see reflections. Glance at windows, shiny cars, trees, and walls. Which things make reflections and which don't?

How Reflections Work

Reflections happen because light **rays** travel in straight lines. That is why you can aim a flashlight at an object to light it up. Light travels in a straight line until it hits another object. When it hits an object, the light is **absorbed** (soaked up) or **reflected**. When light reflects, it bounces off a surface like how a ball bounces off a wall. When a ray of light is reflected from a surface, it changes direction.

When light bounces off a flat, smooth surface such as a calm lake, we can see a clear reflection on the surface.

light

Some surfaces reflect light very well, but others reflect light poorly. Most surfaces are slightly rough. If you look very closely, you can see that even a smooth surface such as a table has little bumps and pits on it. When surfaces are slightly rough, light rays bounce off them in lots of different directions. When objects reflect and **scatter** light in this way, we can see the objects, but we cannot see any clear **images** reflected in their surfaces.

When there are ripples or waves on the surface of a lake, light is scattered in many directions and there are no clear reflections.

light

Activity: Reflecting Materials

Find out which materials **reflect** light best.

What to do

1 Ask an adult to help you cut two eyeholes in the middle of one end of the box. You will look through these holes.

What you need

- scissors
- a large shoebox or file box with a lid
- a small flashlight
- sticky tape
- graph paper
- aluminum foil
- white paper
- black paper.

2 Cut a hole down one side of the box just big enough to poke the flashlight through at an angle, so you can aim it at the far end inside of the box when the lid is on.

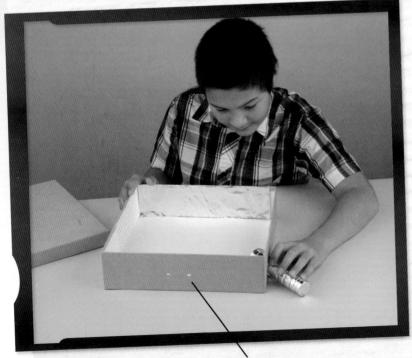

eyeholes

3 On the inside of the box, stick a sheet of graph paper across from the side you will poke the flashlight through.

4 Stick a smooth, flat piece of foil to the inside back of the box, across from your eyeholes. Put the lid on and look through the eyeholes. Shine the flashlight on the foil at an angle, so it reflects light onto the graph paper. Now crumple a piece of foil into a ball and unfold it to repeat the test. What do you notice about the reflected light?

5 Now stick the white and then the black paper at the back of the box, smooth first, then crumpled, one at a time. Repeat the flashlight test. Which materials reflect light best?

What happens?

A smooth, shiny surface such as flat foil reflects light well. The crumpled foil reflects light less well because its surface is no longer smooth. Some of the light is reflected in different directions. The white paper reflects light better than the black paper because black **absorbs** nearly all the light that hits it. Smooth, shiny surfaces reflect light best, and lighter surfaces reflect light better than dark surfaces.

Mirrors

Mirrors are very good at **reflecting**. They reflect most of the light that hits them. Most mirrors are made of very smooth glass with a thin layer of metal on the back. If you put a cup in front of a mirror, light reflects off the cup. When **rays** of light from the cup strike the smooth surface of the mirror, they bounce back at the same angle. Your eyes see these reflected rays as a very clear and sharp **image** of the cup.

We see an image (our **reflection**) in a mirror because its surface is perfectly smooth and shiny.

mirror reflecting sunlight

Amazing mirrors

One town in Norway used to be very dark in winter because it is in a narrow, steep-sided valley that blocks the light. Now there are giant mirrors on a hillside that reflect sunlight down into the town to make it brighter!

The image we see in a mirror is the same as the object that makes it. The difference is that the image is reversed. That's why words look backwards when you hold a book up to a mirror, and why your reflection seems to wave its right hand when you wave your left hand. Try it for yourself!

Activity: Mirrors and Symmetry

Mirrors can help us find **lines of symmetry** of an object and more!

What to do

What you need

- a ruler
- a pen
- sheets of blank paper
- two small mirrors
- sticky tape.

1 Use a ruler to draw a line down the middle of a sheet of blank paper. Draw one half of a funny face on one half of the page, making sure your drawing touches the line in the middle. Now place a mirror on the line with the mirror side facing the **image**. The image should appear on the blank side of the paper. You can complete your face by using the **reflection** as a guide!

2 For this activity, you are going to use the two mirrors to see yourself as others see you, rather than as you look in a mirror. Tape the two small mirrors together along one edge and stand them up like an open book, with the mirrors at right angles to each other. How many reflections do you see? Look into the right-hand mirror at your reflection. What do you notice?

What happens?

If you put the mirror on a line of symmetry, the mirror reflection will complete one whole image of the object. The view in the mirror looks just like the original shape, but flipped. A shape is symmetrical if both sides of it are the same when a mirror line is drawn.

When you look at yourself in the right-hand mirror of the mirror "book," light from the left side of your face hits the left mirror and is **reflected** to the right-hand mirror, which reflects it back to your eye. The same thing happens on the other side of your face. So, you see yourself as others see you, instead of reversed or backwards, as you usually look in a single mirror.

Bending Light

Light is **absorbed** by or **reflects** off most things, but some surfaces make it bend instead! Have you ever noticed how a straw in a glass of water can look bent or broken when you look at it from certain angles? This strange effect happens because water makes light bend or **refract**. Light also refracts when it shines into other dense substances such as glass, plastic, or oil.

The spoon above the water looks normal because light from it travels directly to our eyes. The spoon in the water looks broken because light travels from water to air before hitting our eyes.

Light refracts when it passes from one substance into another substance that changes how fast light travels. It is like the way water slows us down when we try to walk through it. The same thing happens to light when it shines through water. Light **rays** slow down and, as they do so, they change direction.

Trick of light

When we look down into a pond, fish look higher than they really are. That is because the rays of light from the fish are refracted as they leave the water. This tricks our mind into thinking the rays come from an imaginary fish higher in the pond!

image of the fish

real fish

Activity: Light Tricks

Use **refraction** to play tricks with light.

What you need

- a ruler
- a black marker
- thin, white cardboard (postcard size)
- drinking glass
- a jug of water.

What to do

1 Use the ruler and marker to draw a straight line down the center of the long side of the cardboard. The line should divide the cardboard into two equal halves.

2 Stand the glass on the cardboard so that the bottom of the glass lies on top of the line. While looking down into the glass, move it a little until the line appears to divide the bottom of the glass in half.

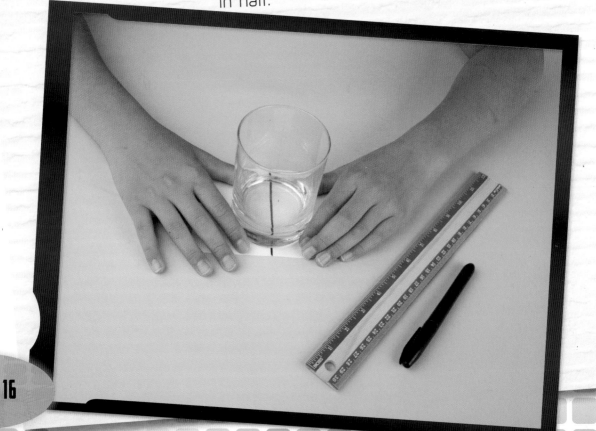

3 Pour some water into the glass while you are looking down into it at the line through the base. Watch what happens to the line through the base of the glass as you add water.

Try this!

Try this trick on your friends. Put a penny at the bottom of a bowl. Tell them to look at it and then to step slowly away. The coin will seem to disappear. Then pour water into the bowl, and the coin will magically appear again, even though it never moves!

What happens?

As you pour water into the glass, the line appears to move to one side. This happens because light slows down when it moves from air into water. When light changes speed, it bends, because one edge of the light **ray** hits the surface and changes speed very slightly before the other edge. This change in direction makes it look as if the line moves.

Seeing Things

We see **light sources**, such as lamps and flashlights, because they give off light. We see most objects because light from a light source **reflects** off objects into our eyes. Light enters the eye through the **pupil**. The pupil is the black hole in the middle of the colored part of the eye called the iris.

Eye muscles

In dim light, **muscles** in the iris pull on the pupil to make it bigger, so it lets in more light to help us see. In bright light, they make the pupil smaller to protect the delicate parts inside your eye.

We see things because light travels from light sources to our eyes or from light sources to objects and then to our eyes.

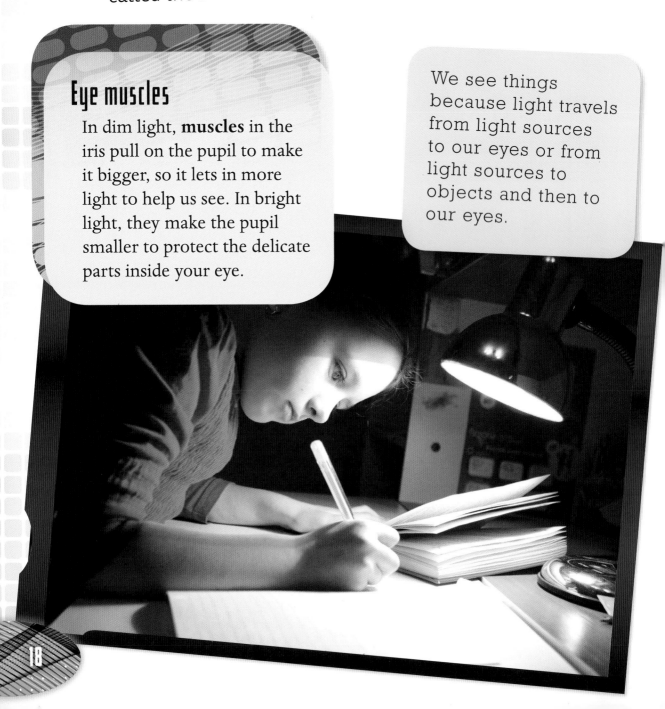

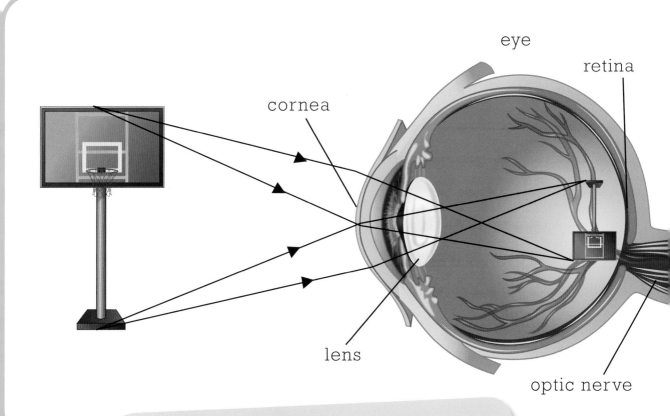

eye

retina

cornea

lens

optic nerve

The cornea, a transparent layer over the eye, **refracts** light together with the lens. The image that hits the retina is upside down, but the brain turns it the right way up again!

After light goes through the pupil into the eye, it passes through a clear, curved part called a **lens**. The lens changes shape to help it focus the clearest **image** onto the **retina**. The retina is the surface at the back of the eye. The retina sends coded messages about what your eyes see to the brain, along the optic nerve.

Activity: Pinhole Camera

Make a pinhole camera.

What to do

1 Take the lid off the shoebox. Paint the inside of your box black and tape over any tiny holes to make sure no light can get into the box once the lid is on.

2 Next, cut two rectangular holes, each about 5 by 3 inches (12 by 8 centimeters) wide, on opposite sides of the box.

3 Cut a piece of black paper that is big enough to stick over one of the holes. Stick it on the inside of the box, making sure it completely covers the hole.

4 Cut a piece of tracing paper that is big enough to stick over the other hole. Stick it on the inside of the box, making sure it completely covers the hole.

What you need

- a shoebox
- black paint and a paintbrush
- sticky tape
- scissors
- ruler
- black paper
- tracing paper
- a thumbtack
- a thick towel.

5 Use the thumbtack to make a small hole in the middle of the black paper. Then put the lid back on the box and tape it down so no light can get in.

6 Now point the pinhole toward something that is in the light, like a tree. Put the towel over your head and the back of the camera to block out the light. What do you notice about the **image** you can see on the tracing paper?

Warning!
Never use your pinhole camera to look at the Sun, since it could hurt your eyes badly.

What happens?
The **rays** of light from the top and bottom of the object you look at cross over as they go through the pinhole and hit the camera screen (the tracing paper). That is why the image you see is upside down. This is what the **retinas** in your eyes see before your brain flips images the right way up.

Looking at Lenses

The **lenses** in your eyes help you see by **refracting** light to focus it onto the **retina**. Lenses in the glasses people wear work in a similar way. These lenses are pieces of transparent (clear) glass or plastic. They make the light that enters the eye change direction slightly, so it seems as if the light comes from nearer or farther away.

The lenses in a pair of glasses refract light to help people who have difficulty seeing things close up or far away.

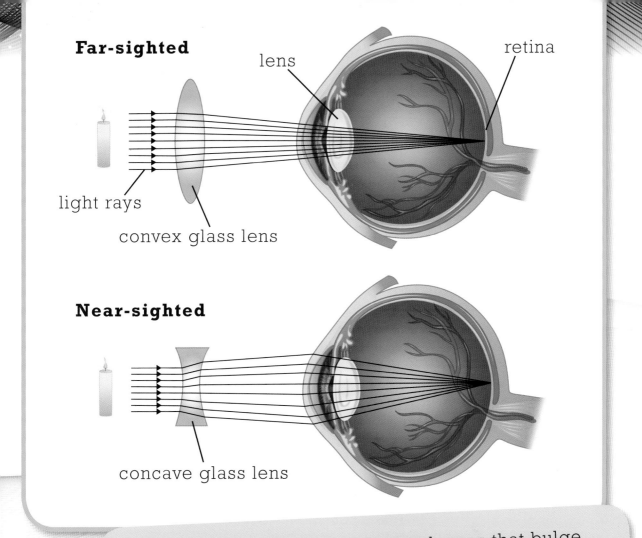

Far-sighted

lens

retina

light rays

convex glass lens

Near-sighted

concave glass lens

Far-sighted people need **convex** lenses that bulge outward in the center to bend light **rays** in and bring them closer together. Near-sighted people use **concave** lenses that curve inward and make light spread out.

People need glasses when an eye lens fails to refract light onto the retina properly. A near-sighted person's lens focuses **images** in front of the retina so he or she only sees nearby things clearly. A far-sighted person's lens focuses images behind the retina so he or she only sees distant things clearly. Far-sighted and near-sighted people need different shaped lenses to bend light in different ways so that light hits the retina. The lenses help them to see clearly.

Activity: Magnifying Lens

Make and test your own **magnifying lens** to help you read words in tiny print.

What to do

1 Use the marker to draw a neat circle on the side of the bottle, at the top. You need to draw the circle exactly where the bottle bulges out.

2 Ask an adult to help you cut out the circle carefully. You have made a **convex** lens.

3 Place the lens on a table so it makes a bowl shape. Carefully add a few drops of water to it, until the middle of the lens is completely covered.

4 Hold your lens over the words in a book. Move it closer or farther away until you can see the words get larger, or magnified.

What happens?

Lenses are curved to **refract**, or bend, light. Magnifying lenses have a convex lens that curves outward on both sides. Your plastic bottle lens curves outward, and the top of your water drop curves outward, too. When you hold this convex lens over a book, it acts as a magnifying glass. It magnifies the letters and words and makes them look bigger.

Light Reflectors

Things that **reflect** light well can be useful. Light **reflectors** keep you safe at night. Cyclists wear special reflective strips on clothing to reflect light from car headlights straight back to the driver. Dark clothing would just **absorb** the light, so drivers would not see them.

Stay safe at night by wearing or carrying things that reflect light. Carry a flashlight and wear light-colored clothes with reflective strips. Be safe and be seen!

Road safety

Road reflectors called cats' eyes reflect car headlights to help drivers see the road ahead. A man got the idea for this invention when the shining eyes of a cat stopped him from driving off a road in the fog!

Convex mirrors inside cars reflect a larger area behind the vehicle than could be seen with the same size flat mirror.

Mirrors are used for more than simple **reflections**. **Concave** mirrors curve or bulge inward toward the middle. They make reflected objects look bigger and closer than they really are. Concave mirrors are used as makeup mirrors or shaving mirrors because they **magnify** things. **Convex** mirrors curve or bulge outward. They make objects look smaller, but they give you a wider view. They are used for rearview mirrors in cars or security mirrors in stores.

Activity: Periscope

Make a periscope and use **reflected** light to see over a wall that is taller than you!

What to do

1 Cut the peaked top off one carton. On the side, at the bottom, cut a small window.

2 Lay the carton on its side so that the window is on the left and facing you. On the top side, in the bottom-left corner, use the protractor to measure 45 degrees. Draw a line at 45 degrees across the top side.

3 Using this line, ask an adult to cut out a slot for the mirror to slide into. Don't cut all the way to the edges.

What you need

- scissors
- two clean, dry, and empty milk or juice cartons
- a protractor
- a pencil
- two rectangular hand mirrors
- sticky tape.

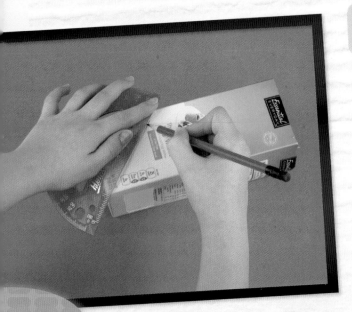

Warning!

Try to use plastic, unbreakable mirrors. If you can't, be careful.

4 Slide your mirror into the slot. The reflecting side of the mirror should face the window.

5 Hold the carton up and look through the window. You should see the ceiling. Tape the mirror in place.

6 Repeat steps 1 to 5 with the second carton. Then stand one carton so its window faces you. Stand the other carton on top of it with the window facing away from you. Slide the top carton just inside the bottom carton and tape them together.

7 Look through the bottom window. You should be able to see what is going on out of the top window!

What happens?

Light **reflects** away from a mirror at the same angle that it hits a mirror. The mirrors in a periscope are at angles, so when light from the outside hits the top mirror, it reflects to the lower mirror. Then the light reflects into your eye so you can see the **image** from the top mirror.

Glossary

absorb to soak up or take in something

concave shape that curves or bulges in toward the center

convex shape that curves or bulges outward

image copy of an object formed by light

lens curved part that focuses light. There is a lens in each of our eyes. The lenses in glasses are curved glass or plastic that make things look bigger, smaller, or clearer.

light source something that makes or gives off light

line of symmetry imaginary line where you could fold the image and have both halves match exactly

magnify make things appear bigger

muscle body part that makes other body parts move

pupil tiny opening in the center of the iris in the eye that looks black

ray narrow line or beam of light

reflect bounce back light

reflection image that gets pointed back at you by a smooth, shiny surface

reflector thing that is useful because it reflects or bounces back light in a specific direction

refract bend light rays as they pass from one kind of material (such as water) to another (such as air)

refraction bending of light

retina part at the back of the eye that sends messages about what your eyes see to the brain

scatter reflect light in all directions

Find Out More

Books

Ballard, Carol. *Exploring Light* (How Does Science Work?). New York: PowerKids, 2008.

Claybourne, Anna. *Secrets of Light* (Science Secrets). New York: Marshall Cavendish Benchmark, 2011.

Hewitt, Sally. *Light* (Amazing Science). New York: Crabtree, 2008.

Riley, Peter. *Light* (The Real Scientist Investigates). N. Mankato, Minn.: Sea-to-Sea, 2011.

Web sites

Facthound offers a safe, fun way to find Internet sites related to this book. All of the sites on Facthound have been researched by our staff.

Here's all you do:

Visit www.facthound.com

Type in this code: 9781410979438

Index